Marshall, Sr.

Committed L.O.V.E.

The Four Cornerstones of a Happier Marriage

All Biblical passages from the New International version.
All definitions taken from The American Heritage Dictionary of the English Language, Fourth Edition, © 2006 by Houghton Mifflin Company unless otherwise noted.

Written by Quintin L. Marshall, Sr. with Kate E. Stephenson

First published in 2009, by Welstar Publications, Inc.
628 Lexington Avenue, Brooklyn, NY 11221
Phone: 718/453-6557, Fax: 718/338-1454
E-mail: drbatson@optonline.net
or editor@welstarpublications.com
ISBN: 978-0-93850310-1

Editing by
Anathaleo S. Blake

Book Design/Typography by
Kate E. Stephenson
Text set in Book Antiqua

Cover Design by
Clive Williamson
OnTarget Communication

This book is dedicated to my beautiful wife Queen, the cornerstone of my deepest affection and love. To our deceased, awesome parents Herman and Arnell Marshall and Beviley and Rosetta Lane; without their marriage examples we would not be enjoying the life that we now live. To my deceased oldest brother Herman Jr., one of the greatest gospel witnesses I have ever known. To my big sister Jo Anne, the best big sister in the whole wide world – I love you without limits. To my other talented siblings: Linda, Steve and Dondre. To my six sons and daughters and their mates who hold the mantle of our legacy. To Aunt Mozel, the best aunt in the whole human race.

To the New Life Tabernacle church family, that has allowed me to pastor to them for the past 20 years.

And foremost to God, the author and finisher of my faith, to whom belongs all the glory and the praise in my life for all the things that he has done amongst us as the children of men.

To all, I say thank you for believing and supporting me in this kingdom work.

Sincerely,

Supt. Quintin L. Marshall, Sr.

"Love is friendship that has caught fire.
It is quiet understanding,
mutual confidence, sharing and forgiving.
It is loyalty through good and bad times.
It settles for less than perfection and
makes allowances for human weaknesses."

~ Ann Landers

Contents

Introduction

The Four Cornerstones of L.O.V.E.

---

1 Corinthians 13:1-8,13

*[1]If I speak in the tongues of men and of angels,
but have not love, I am only a resounding gong or a
clanging cymbal. [2]If I have the gift of prophecy and
can fathom all mysteries and all knowledge, and if I
have a faith that can move mountains, but have not
love, I am nothing. [3]If I give all I possess to the poor
and surrender my body to the flames, but have not
love, I gain nothing.*

*[4]Love is patient, love is kind. It does not envy, it
does not boast, it is not proud. [5]It is not rude, it is not
self-seeking, it is not easily angered, it keeps no record
of wrongs. [6]Love does not delight in evil but rejoices
with the truth. [7]It always protects, always trusts,
always hopes, always perseveres.*

*[8]Love never fails. But where there are prophecies,
they will cease; where there are tongues, they will be
stilled; where there is knowledge, it will pass away.*

*[13]And now these three remain: faith, hope and
love. But the greatest of these is love.*

Commitment vs. Involvement

*In a breakfast of eggs and bacon,
the chicken was involved but the pig was committed.*

Enduring Love is a many splendid thing, and a culmination of much committed HARD WORK. It takes work to maintain any relationship borne out of love. In this race to win the ultimate prize of enduring, all-encompassing, ever-conquering LOVE, we must be life-givingly committed like the pig at breakfast, and not merely egg-laying involved like the chicken.

One of the greatest blessings God bestowed upon us is the power to love one another—the ability to recognize ourselves in others, and to seek our highest potential by joining with one another in the union of marriage; and while it's rewards can be awesomely satisfying, satanic challenges from the Devil can be great. The Lord never guaranteed the road in marriage would always be smooth and that our feet would always be steady. Life itself is a stark reminder to us that nothing worthwhile ever comes easily.

But God never leaves us alone, either. As in many areas of life, there are methods to understanding and solving our problems—tools to help us towards remodeling the road, repairing the potholes and relaying the asphalt so that our feet may once again step sure. In the College of Love, there are three major courses:

Love 101: Understanding the love of God the Father, God the Son, and God the Holy Ghost for Yourself

Love 201: Understanding the Love of God in You

Love 301: Understanding the Love of God You Must Convey to Your Mate—a Reflection of You

To begin schooling in love, you must start at the foundation. It is only through a greater knowledge of and relationship with God and our Savior Jesus Christ that we can truly come to know ourselves and the gift of love. Without understanding the Almighty source of love, we cannot see it within ourselves, nor can we give it outwards to others.

This deeper connection with God will bring you to the next level—a deeper connection with yourself. Our conceptions of ourselves govern everything we do, say, think and feel. We react to the world and all of

God's creation based upon our own understandings of love. If we know and believe ourselves to be children of God, accepting His grace and love into our hearts, then we can know and believe in the God within us. When we connect with our inner spirit of Godliness, then we are truly able to love.

When we have discovered this ability to love, we are set on a path towards the *one* we will love. The Bible tells us that it is good and right to partner with another, to be equally yoked and fruitful in the covenant of marriage. To love each other in this way is to honor and love the Lord. He made man as a reflection of Himself, then He made woman as a reflection of man. By looking upon each other, we can come into a greater understanding of both ourselves and of the God who made us. By loving each other, we commit ourselves to not only each other, but to the God from whom all love springs.

If you have arrived at this book, it is my sincere hope that you have invested the time and attention to the study of both God and yourself, first. In order to engage in a committed love, we must first commit to learning ourselves and the Lord.

I always tell my young congregants that if you haven't discovered your own worth, then you can't recognize anyone else's. If you feel you have little value, you will allow yourself to be bought for a value meal price. When your mate can buy you for the price of a value meal, it is more likely that s/he may be able to afford several others—one in the morning, one in the afternoon, and another at night.

But if you know and feel the intrinsic value of all that God has given you to share with your mate, you will require a full investment of love. S/he will only be able to afford one purchase of love in *you*. A marriage is an investment of everything you've got. Discover your own value and your value to God. Do not skip this step.

Skipping steps often leads to busted knees and lips, and broken hearts and lives. Often the price of failure in marriage is paid by innocent bystanders, not merely the separating or divorcing couple. Divorce is a tragic event, for the couples, for the families, for churches, and for communities.

Some wonder why people still get married at all, when it seems like such a gamble—a coin toss (researchers agree that approximately half of all marriages wind up in divorce, according to divorcerate.org). But it's the lack of educated commitment that leads to this high volume malfunction and the continuing cycle of casual involvements. Ill-prepared and ill-informed about ourselves and relationship building, we too often enter unions we are unequipped to handle.

It is difficult to perceive what a healthy marriage is when surrounded by the residue of divorce; when our mothers and fathers leave this earth without sharing with us their mistakes and their triumphs; when marriages don't thrive, but merely exist; when our mentors are celebrities who change spouses like they change hairstyles; when we rush into our hormones, instead of thinking with our logic and feeling with our hearts. How can we expect to know how to succeed in our relationships?

I understand the difficulties firsthand. It was the failure of divorce that led me to the four cornerstones of committed love. Looking back, I recognized a selfishness within myself, an unwillingness to learn about and grow with my mate, and a lack of commitment to all the facets of my marriage. And when the final papers were signed, I looked around and saw the expansive reach and devastation of my failure.

In response to my prayerful and sincere desire to learn from these past mistakes, the Lord spoke to me about the four cornerstones to building a happier marriage. The four cornerstones are:

1. Learn your mate
2. Overcome obstacles with your mate
3. Value your mate, and
4. Escape with your mate

The Lord gave me an understanding of these ideas so that I could succeed when I found the love of my life and the heart of my soul, my wife, Queen, of twelve years now.

These cornerstones helped me establish a solid foundation upon which to build our marriage, and I have shared them with many others in casual conversation, counseling, and seminar courses. It is my desire to give to others what the Lord so graciously gave to me—a sweet serenity and living love with my mate.

These four cornerstones, grounded in positive actions, can help make your marriage that much more inviting for your mate. These major positive actions are important elements of the cornerstones. They include: Communication, Prioritization, Education, and Evolution. These elements make the difference between just being married and having a happy, committed, healthy relationship that will continue to grow as you do.

1) Communication is listening openly and speaking with understanding; it is the key to all relationships, be it with a spouse, children, co-workers , or strangers on the street. It is difficult to get through life successfully without becoming an effective communicator. Being able to express inner thoughts, aspirations, and common daily necessities is an important part of everyday living. If you can't speak your needs, how can you expect anyone else to fulfill them?

2) Prioritization is the act of putting things in the correct order by importance—knowing who and what is most important in your life. If things are out of order in your life, it is difficult to get on the right track and stay on it. When things are out of order, your mind isn't right, your body is out of whack, and your spirit fades. That's why you've got to prioritize correctly. Remember to put God first in all things; second, get yourself together; and then, serve your mate before and forsaking all others. If you are not establishing this order in your life, your life will be established in chaos.

3) Education is the continued learning of yourself, your mate, and God. We often take this process for granted or undervalue it. The adages "A mind is a terrible thing to waste" and "It's never too late to learn" are cliché because they are true. Education is essential to growth. And the most important lessons are learning yourself, your God, and your mate.

4) Evolution is the process of change, usually for the better. When we embrace change,

it can become a helpmate rather than a hindrance. When we think of evolution as moving from who we were to the better person we are going to be, we can understand the higher plans God has for us. It is never God's plan for you to stay the way you are; if that were the case we would not have life stages—birth, infancy, childhood, adolescence, adulthood, and old age—we would just stay babies forever. And just as we change, get older, mature, and hopefully become wiser, so do the others around us. Allowing them to change as we allow ourselves to change is a blessing and a gift.

Through better communication, proper prioritization, informed education and by embracing evolution, you will better understand and interact with yourself, your mate, and the world around you.

I invite you to walk into a better way of living and giving, through a stronger relationship and knowledge of God's love. Let's talk about committed L.O.V.E.

1. L – Learn Your Mate

Continuing Education

Proverbs 22: 6

Train a child in the way he should go,
and when he is old he will not turn from it

If you think education is expensive, try ignorance.
~Attributed to Andy McIntyre & Derek Bok

Like constructing a good house, the key to building a strong and enduring marriage is to lay a solid foundation. The foundation to a happy marriage is supported by four cornerstones:

1. Learn Your Mate
2. Overcome With Your Mate
3. Value Your Mate, and
4. Escape with Your Mate

No matter what winds blow from the North, South, East or West, the four corners of your marriage will be stable if grounded with these cornerstones. In this chapter, we want to talk about Learning Your Mate.

It is a fact that people will invest years of study to be judges, lawyers, teachers, or preachers, putting in dozens of years of schooling to establish careers. But sometimes, we put so little study time into developing the higher relationships that we seek. Our first priority should be to study ourselves in relation to the Lord—this being an eternal covenant. But then, we have to study our evolving mates—the marriage union being a commitment until death.

The vows of marriage are similar to our covenant with God. It is a parallel contract that signals the earthly allegiance of one human being to another, the creation of one unit formed by two beings. Taking this into account, marriage is a state to be entered into soberly, with discretion and understanding. It is worthy of the same intense investment and study needed for the SATs, a college degree, or the bar exam.

Ideally, the act of learning your mate should come before marriage. Take the time to court and woo, as well as learn the likes and dislikes, goals and dreams, family and personal history of your mate. There should be no rush when you want to spend the rest of your life with that special person.

However, sometimes we just get caught up. We find ourselves in something before we have fully investigated the situation. And that's okay, because it's never too late to learn. This chapter is for everyone—those fishing and those already caught in the net.

First, let's get this out of the way. Both men *and* women are guilty of skipping this step. The Bible tells us about the first lesson in learning your mate, Adam and Eve.

In Genesis 3, Adam, Eve and the serpent are all out in the garden. But while Adam is out tending the garden, the serpent is busy watching Eve. The serpent takes notes on how Eve walks and talks. He takes notes on how she associates with Adam. He watches everything that she does. And, the serpent doesn't just jump out and speak to her—he waits until it's the right time and she's in the right mood, and then he talks up on her.

The serpent whispers to Eve while her husband is just out of earshot. That serpent sweet-talks Eve into doing something Adam had expressly told her *not* to do—while Adam is just a few feet away! (*That's like another man taking your wife while you are standing there* watching *him do it.*) The serpent studied Eve, until he understood everything about her, including how to manipulate her into doing his biding.

Not only manipulating her but after convincing her to eat from the forbidden tree, the serpent turned around and said "By the way, since you've already done what Adam told you not to do, why don't you get Adam to do it too?" And Eve does just that.

The serpent's attentiveness and Adam's distraction lead to the temptation of Eve and the fall of man. Had Adam studied his mate as closely as the serpent, perhaps we would all now be frolicking happily in the bounty of Eden. *Perhaps*. But surely, the serpent would have had to resort to more cunning efforts to lure Eve.

Now we could blame Eve for messing up, but men *too* have fallen victim. The studying of your mate is a powerful tool in understanding the inner-workings of your relationship. But in the hands of a vampire mate—the kind of mate who sucks and bleeds you of all that is healthy and alive within you, of all of the love and laughter, kindness and support, of all that makes you the person you are—the consequences of this study can be deadly. Take, for instance, Samson and Delilah.

Judges 16: 4–22 tells us how Delilah got to know Samson too well, discovering his greatest weakness and using it for ill gains. Delilah understood what many Christian women don't—she studied Sampson. She interrogated Samson until she got him to do what he wouldn't have done with anyone else. She rubbed his head, his arms, and his shoulders until she found the right spot, pushed the right button and he told her what she wanted to know. He finally gave her the key to his strength—a feat no one else had been able to achieve—that his strength came from his hair.

Sometimes it is a scary thing to become vulnerable, to open up and give up the key to ourselves. We fear the serpents and Delilahs of the world. But when we learn our mates, when both parties are equally committed to understanding each other, it becomes a great comfort. When we know they are upset without asking, when we understand their unique habits, their needs and desires, we can bring strength to our mates.

For instance, I know when my wife is cold in the bed. It's a certain way that she lays. So I grab the blanket and cover her up because part of my assignment as her life-mate is to protect her, even from the cold. To protect her, to look out for her, to shelter her from anything that I think might hurt her or take away from her. I stand in the gap for her. It's part of my assignment. And she stands behind me and supports me, standing in the gaps for me. We are each others shield and road warriors, because we have come into an understanding of each other. We have learned each other to such a degree that we speak each others thoughts and finish each others sentences.

Individual Pasts—Collective Futures

My wife and I still have our battles, and it is a continuing education as we change daily. This knowledge has not come easily. But because we have taken the time to get to know each other, our flaws and imperfections, our strengths and accomplishments, our storied pasts and envisioned goals for the future, our union grows stronger everyday. In knowing each others pasts, the key to understanding the future is gained.

While the present is a gift, don't get so caught up in the now that you miss the sneak preview of the future. Men, they used to say if you want to know if a woman will be acceptable to you in 20 - 30 years, look at her mother. Ladies, look at the father. The same DNA that is in the mother and the father is also in the person with whom you are in a relationship. The influence our families have on us cannot be denied. We are a product of our families for better or worse, and there is no escaping it. So right now, be honest with yourself. It is difficult enough to have a rocky relationship with the in-laws, but it's scary to realize ten years down the road that you are also married to them.

I'm not saying there aren't exceptions to every rule, but be honest in your intentions and expectations. If your values are not the same as your mate's today, don't think they will be tomorrow. If you have never taken the time to evaluate, inspect and compare your values, do not be surprised when you bump heads when the sticky issues of money, children and intimacy become important.

People will try to learn each other while they are dating, although oftentimes, males and females have different goals in mind. Guys often have their minds targeted on the flesh, while their counterparts may be focused on finding a husband.

This may seem old-fashioned, but men, you may not realize that from the time of girlhood, many women dream of having a husband, of having a protectorate—it's the Cinderella Syndrome. You may laugh, but in the hearts of many women is this vision of their lives. Unfortunately, there are a whole lot of Princes that aren't Charming. (And for men thinking to find their own personal princess, sometimes instead of Cinderella what you get is the Wicked Witch.)

Bombarded with images and messages of sex, moral latitude, and rampant infidelity, young men at a certain stage of their lives are looking for a good time. While, on the other hand, young women, perhaps also interested in a good time, may also have one eye on the future and building a family. This starts a disconnect at the very beginning of a relationship.

Inherently, this difference in our approaches and goals for dating can lead to difficulties. If you are learning only what is necessary to have a good time in the flesh, you will find yourself at a loss when the flame has burned out. If you are learning only what is necessary to get yourself down the aisle, but not enough to know the soul of the person you are marrying, you may wake up after the honeymoon is over wondering, *Who did I marry?*

Learn your mate's needs and wants. Do you know if your mate wants children? Is s/he grounded in the church? Is s/he family-oriented or distanced from relations? What is this person's background? Do you have similar internal values and outlooks on life? If you have not asked yourself these questions, you have not educated yourself on your mate.

You don't have to be twins, attached at the brain, with matching wants, desires, and needs. You just need to have a similar concept of destiny. You may not agree on the path, but as long as you agree on the destination, you've won half the battle.

The College of Commitment

Just as the education should not begin directly before the altar, it should not end there either. Marriage is a long-term learning process. From the time we are little, we are in a training session. When mommy and daddy teach their sons not to hit the girls, to take out the trash and mow the lawn, they are instilling some of the husbandly duties of domestic life. When parents teach their little girls to tend the house and be caregivers, they are imparting some of the wifely duties of domestic life. Some of us receive more training than others in these early stages of life.

The next level of learning finds us in the beginning stages of dating and courtship, when we discover how to talk with and relate to members of the opposite sex. Serious courtship, where we learn about our mate's past, usually progresses to marriage. But even after the wooing is over, when we have learned what we can about what has come before marriage, there is still more to learn.

It can take a lifetime to discover all of the likes and dislikes of your partner, to unearth his or her emotions and sensitivities. And in this process of discovery, we may discover more about ourselves. Marriage is the commitment to this continual discovery. Enjoying each other and finding entertainment in each other's company may prove informative. Taking the time to talk with your mate, to escape with them, to hear how they are feeling on any given day about any particular topic, will reveal more insight into who they are. And how you react to their disclosures may reveal more of who you are, in turn.

Problems are bound to happen. We cannot know everything about any person, not even our mates. There are things that are painful, humiliating, and shameful; your mate may be reluctant to share these events even after years of being together. We all have those moments that we keep buried down deep, hoping no one else will ever see them or need to know. But sometimes, those things that we try to keep hidden impact important life decisions. In times of uncertainty and trouble, when your mate's reasons seem mysterious and irrational, seek out answers and solutions in understanding, not in anger.

When your mate is shy about nakedness in

front of you, consider there may be a deeper reason for this inhibition. The reason could be as common as s/he is self-conscious, or as complex and debilitating as a history of child abuse or rape. When your mate is seemingly stingy with money, consider the possible cause. Was your mate's childhood challenging because of a lack of financial stability? Did s/he experience tragedy because of a monetary deficiency?

Our perceptions of ourselves can also cause friction in a relationship. Mama's boys and Daddy's little girls may know what I'm talking about here. There is nothing wrong with having high self-esteem and self-confidence, but sometimes those qualities run to extremes. Instead of having self-confidence, we can be self-centered. Instead of exuding self-esteem, we may project arrogance. And sometimes, instead of being caring and compassionate, we are clingy and needy.

My life is one of sacrifice, but I had to go through stages to realize that was my purpose. Before marrying my wife, I was so selfish. I wanted everything my way and I just couldn't see it anybody else's. But by being married to this wonderful woman, I learned more from her about myself, because I focused on learning her more than any other woman I've known in my whole life. I was totally focused on understanding her. When I learned her, I realized her worth as a virtuous woman—that she was far more valuable than any jewel I could ever purchase for her. I know that there is nothing too good for my wife. If I have to give everything that I have to make her happy, then it's worth it.

But I had to be willing to step outside and beyond myself in order to fully commit to being the person my wife needed me to be. I had to let go of many of my own stubborn ways in order to incorporate her as an equal partner in my life. And that meant letting my own selfishness and foolish pride go to the wayside.

Many things make a person who they are. With the joys of marriage also come the difficulties, and with the discovery of our mate's goodness and great abilities also comes an understanding of their flaws and failings—and an understanding of our own.

If we can understand why we are the way we are, we can better serve each other. With information comes understanding. Take for instance okra. Yes, okra.

My wife loves fried okra, but I hate it! When I was a kid, before I could chew it up, it had already slipped down my throat. I thought of okra as that nasty, slippery stuff and I built up a wall against it. Now my wife—she can tear some okra up, but not me.

We have come to understand each other. Although my wife loves this food, she doesn't try to push her choice on me. And if there is something she doesn't like, I don't push it on her either.

We respect each other's boundaries because we have come to understand each other and the reasons for our likes and dislikes. We may challenge each other to try new things, to expand our horizons; but with an understanding of our tolerance, we don't push each other beyond our reasonable limits. We have learned how far to push each other and when to back off. But through gentle prodding and loving giving, we have grown in our likes by adopting each others'.

Change is Gonna Come

The only true constant is change. God made it such that as the earth rotates on its axis, the seasons of the land change—winter gives way to spring, then bursts into summer and fades into autumn, to return again to the slumber of winter. We are always in a season of change. Our government leaders change with elections, our skin changes with sunlight and age, our bodies grow and our minds expand. Change happens. There is no stopping change, and change is good.

Just like everything else under the sun, our mates will change just as we ourselves change. So don't pigeonhole yourself or your mate. Allow the change to happen and accept it as a natural progression of life. Your mate may have been young and fit when you met, but twenty years down the road gravity catches up with us all. Her memory might have kept you on target when you were both young, but the mind will be challenged as the years roll on, and you just may need to keep your own calendar.

Grey hairs will grow, love handles may develop, personalities may alter, tastes will mature, desires may blossom, needs might change, and all of that is natural and necessary. There is no alternative to change but death.

So if you think your mate will look exactly the same, smell exactly the same, act exactly the same, think exactly the same as when you first met them, then you must think you are *exactly* the same as well. And if you look in the mirror today and see the same person you were ten years ago, you are either in a time warp or denial. But if you accept that you are a being of God who changes and grows with each trial and tribulation that the Lord helps you overcome, then you must also accept that your mate will and does change also. Love them anyway—love them because of it.

Allow yourself to release your selfishness and embrace the positivity of change. Change is a blessing; without it we could not become the disciples God calls us to be. Without change we could not become the best possible incarnations of ourselves. Without change we would all be incapable of salvation and the promise of eternal life. But through Jesus and the Holy Spirit, God works miracles in and through us. He gives us the change needed to improve our communities, our families, ourselves. Change is what gives us the ability to overcome our obstacles, reach our goals and set our sights on higher heights.

2. *O – Overcome with Your Mate*
Hurdling the Obstacles

Hebrews 10: 39; 11: 1

39 But we are not of those who shrink back and are destroyed, but of those who believe and are saved.

1 Now faith is being sure of what we hope for and certain of what we do not see.

When you plant lettuce, if it does not grow well, you don't blame the lettuce. You look for reasons it is not doing well. It may need fertilizer, or more water, or less sun. You never blame the lettuce.

Yet if we have problems with our friends or our family, we blame the other person. But if we know how to take care of them, they will grow well, like the lettuce. Blaming has no positive effect at all, nor does trying to persuade using reason and argument. That is my experience. If you understand, and you show that you understand, you can love, and the situation will change.

~Thich Nhat Hanh

Overcoming with your mate simply means finding solutions that match the dynamic of your marriage. Hurdling obstacles means implementing solutions, rather than obsessing over problems. Changing your mode of thinking from one of antagonism to one of teamwork can be difficult. But to hurdle the obstacles you have to get your mind right.

When you have a hurdle, you have to remember to raise your leg and go over it—not run into it! The race is not given to the swift, nor the battle to the strong, but victory is about enduring until the end. We don't all have the same pace, but we all have the same race. It's the race from life to death; however, short or long it is for each one of us, the vow from Christ is "Be faithful until death and I will give you a crown." The vows of marriage are to be faithful unto death. They are the same.

When we look at marriage, we may ask, "What is faith? What does it mean to be faithful?" *Faith* is the substance of being soulful and the evidence of things not seen. *Faithful* is to be *full* of belief that this marriage is going to make it—that you will do whatever it takes, make every sacrifice to make your marriage work.

What is the greatest obstacle to overcome? Truthfully, our greatest obstacle is often ourselves. Sometimes people allow their egos to get in the way of progress. But that is a no-no when it comes to overcoming obstacles. If you really want to overcome, you have to think outside of your own box. You have to think of things and ways that are matched with your situation and the persons involved.

What are the most common hurdles for couples? The top three are the oldest sources of friction known to man: children, sex, and money.

Yes, our children are often our greatest joy, but the question of *how* to raise those children can also be a bone of deep contention. Differences in upbringing may lead parents to feel differently about what is appropriate and what is inappropriate in childrearing. When these beliefs clash, a storm of discontent will blow in the house for both the parents and the children. And happiness cannot thrive under such intense cloud cover.

I always counsel couples to discuss childrearing before the babies are born, because the issue *will* come up. Methods of discipline are not the same in all households or for all people. When you don't agree on discipline, especially corporal punishment, it can be a source of resentment.

When one parent declares to another, "That's *my* child! You can't do such and such to *my* child," a divide forms in the relationship and the household. Children may take advantage of this discord between parents, using it to get away with their own whims and wants. At the best of times, children are skilled at pushing the boundaries to test what they can get away with; but when a situation has soured and you need the support of your mate, there can be serious repercussions when you cannot come to a resolution for raising the children. When you need the help of your mate, they may well say, "That's *your* child." The stakes may be much greater this time; before you were arguing about discipline, now you may be trying bail your child out of jail. Attitudes have repercussions which we cannot always foresee. But when you set up a cycle of understanding and cooperation, instead of antagonism, you can count on that spirit to see you through the trials and tribulations of life.

Similarly, physical intimacy can be a balm to troubled spirits, but it can also be the source of trouble. When two people are not equally matched in this area, there will be discord and stress. And when the appetites of one outpace those of the other, fidelity and faithfulness may be compromised.

If you know your husband or wife is a lusty person with powerful needs, I counsel spouses to feed them until they are full, then, feed them again to make sure the eye won't even *think* about wondering to another meal. There is no shame in fulfilling your spouse's fantasies; but don't be surprised if someone else does, when you refuse.

Also, how you thought at eighteen is not how you are going to think at forty-eight. The childish things you did as a teenager, you wouldn't dream of doing years later. Your perspective and experience have taught you those activities are not suitable for you. Information changes attitudes and attitudes change actions. How you thought about and engaged in intimacy with one partner may not be profitable with the next. And your own needs and desires may also change over time. Whereas at one time deep kisses might have been your thing, now soft butterfly kisses float your boat. It is important to be attentive to these changing desires in yourself and your mate.

Remember, your mate should be the one to turn you on and vice versa. When the fire cools, you have a hurdle to jump. Don't just accept that the thrill is gone. Rediscover it! We'll talk about that more when we talk about escaping with your mate in chapter four.

Last is the issue of green. Money is a resource, but when it is the source of dispute, it can make enemies out of friends and lovers. Wherever there is too much or too little, problems will arise. And sometimes even when you have just enough, the mismanagement or seeming mismanagement of funds can have a devastating impact on a family.

Money and distrust are common bedfellows. Inviting an open and transparent relationship with your partner when it comes to the family funds can quell many an argument. Especially in tough economies, when jobs are lacking, promotions don't mean more money, and bonuses are on suspension, money issues are particularly challenging. Tensions caused by the lack of status or the tightness of your family budget are often difficult to overcome. Money is a fact of life and the motivator of our economy. But when times get rough, look to each other and call on the higher power that is Jesus Christ to help you through it as a couple.

Sometimes we judge love on how many carats are in the ring, or how many pairs of shoes your partner buys you, or if your partner keeps you in the latest in fashion and bling. The focus on material items that money can buy may blind us to more important factors. *How would you feel about this person if money were not a factor?* Is it the *person* that is important to you or the *things* s/he gives you? These are the important questions to ask yourself; if you find the material more important than the person, your priorities may not be in order and your status as life-mates is on the rocks. A little re-education may be in order.

But, if you know your mate and have learned them well, you have already conquered more than half the battle. We can reduce the obstacles, by doing our homework. Know and respect your differences, work *with* your mate, and operate in solutions-based thinking. We can do these things by recognizing and appreciating our differences, prioritizing our battles, making concessions and refusing to let the argument win. We're going to talk about each of these in the next sections. First, let's address our differences.

Valuing Difference

Sometimes in marriage, we don't take into account that we come from different backgrounds. We think all the world is like the world we came from. Anyone who acts differently than we do, that has a different set of values than we do, we think that they are abnormal. But while we are looking at other folks thinking they are crazy, they are looking back at us thinking the same thing. They think you are crazy too.

So when people marry quickly without getting to know the roots of their mate, they get confused. When you don't know the roots of the tree, you may not understand the fruit that it bears. Many times you may think you have an orange tree, when in fact, you've really got a pear tree. Or you think you have an apple tree, and you really have a mango tree. Or you think you have a mango tree and what you've really got is a coconut tree. So you treat the tree like what you *think* it is, then you are surprised when the fruit is not what you expected.

Let's look at it from another angle. In the olden days, some of ya'll might still do this—

the moms would take the fruit from the tree, and cook that fruit down, throw in some sugar, until it got all tender and mushy. We called that preserves. When times got rough and the syrup ran out, mom would pull that jar down and spread those preserves over your bread, and, man, were you thankful. But when you are trying to cook a coconut like you cook an apple or a pear, it won't come out the same and it won't preserve properly. You might get something too sweet, mushy and overdone, or maybe the fruit will be bitter, hard and tough. But the Bible says you know the tree by the fruit that it bears.

When we say we want to learn a person and overcome obstacles with a person, we also have to understand the environment from which they come, understand the type of fruit they produce. Because when it comes to overcoming obstacles, we have to start thinking solutions verses thinking problems. And we have to understand that different is *not* abnormal, different is *not* incorrect, different is *not* wrong. Different is just that—different. But if we learn from our differences and accept them as an integral part of each other, we can adjust the ways in which we approach situations.

Your mate's fruit may be different: it may take longer for his temper to boil; it may take less time for her understanding to dawn; you may require less sugar because your approach is so sweet; or you may be ready to tackle certain challenges because the spark in your belly keeps the fires burning hot. We can better overcome the problems that will arise if we understand that difference can be a strength. Using these differences to gain victory in every battle, allowing your mate to take the lead when his or her strengths are best suited for the situation, realizing when to speak up and when to back down, and how to balance each other in times of difficulty—these are learned behaviors. They are learned by properly caring for and understanding the type of person your mate is.

But sometimes in relationships, problems can be more than just differences. It may seem like one person is giving more than the other; like one side is being cheated. In 2 Corinthians 6:14 we are told, "Be not unequally yoked." It is this unequal yoking that may be the root of your problem.

When I met my wife, she was so used to the people who had been in her life treating her like a queen; but the men did not act like kings. She was given much, but not asked to give anything in return. I was different. If I sow into your ground, I expect a harvest. Because the Bible says that if I sow then I shall also reap. And, I don't have an expectation of a one-way relationship. In marriage, both parties have to work together as a team, because the harvest of a marriage is dependent upon the sowing abilities of both members of the couple.

If everyone wants a bountiful harvest, then everyone has to plant a bountiful seed. It's amazing what you can do when you plant seeds, instead of eating them. The return on investment is totally different. But there are four determinates of how the seed will bloom:

1) There must be a planter to release the seed. You have to be willing to give, and turn the seed loose in order to allow the seed to take root and grow. You have to give up a part of yourself in order to nurture the seed into a seedling and then into a growing plant.

2) The ground has to be ready to receive

the seed. The Bible says that when the man had sown the seed all the ground was not ready to receive it. Some of the ground was stony, and some of the soil was shallow. When the wind came it blew the seed away, because the ground could not hold it. But some was ready to receive it and had the potential to bring forth a bountiful crop.

3) The seed has to match the ground in which you are planting it. If the seed is not compatible with the earth and the environment in which it is planted, it will not grow.

4) God, when He decides things are done the right way, gives an increase to the bounty.

In marriage, we have to create an atmosphere of love and understanding in which to plant the seeds; then we have to devotedly tend to the seeds; and we have to understand what kind of seeds we are growing. If we are going to overcome obstacles, we have to sow some forgiveness seed, some mercy seed, compassion seed, confidence seed, generosity seed—love seeds. When we begin to sow those seeds, then we will see that bounty come back to us.

The Anthill and the Mountain

There are high and low hurdles that we have to face. After understanding and creating common ground with our mates, one of the first things we have to do in facing problems is determine what rank these obstacles get. If something is of small significance than we should not give it a great deal of attention. If it is of great importance then it should not be at the bottom of the list. Prioritizing is the key to conquering our problems.

When we talk about low hurdles, we are talking about simple things, like "Honey, you drank all the milk and put the empty carton back in the fridge," or "You used all of the sweetener, but I needed some for my coffee." Those are the kinds of things that people can go off on. They won't sleep in the same bed for weeks because of small altercations like these.

When we become polarized over the minor, we use up the energy we could be using on the major. We choke on a gnat, and miss the elephant sitting on the hood of the car. It is amazing how so many couples have been ruined by small issues being made large, and large issues being made small. Marriages can be torn apart by a simple thing—something that a small thought and a tiny concession could have solved.

Many times couples fight over the same issues for years because they don't conquer them. They don't face the cause of their, most often small, frictions because neither side wants to listen. Each wants to voice an opinion, but no one wants to hear anyone else's. You find that folk are yelling at each other, not always because they have something new to say. Rather, they are yelling because they think what they are saying is not being heard. So they shout louder. But while they're shouting, the other person tunes them out. So the shoutin' and the fussin' is generally done in vain.

The Bible says, "A soft answer will turn away wrath" and "come let us reason together." As we get older, hopefully, we learn how to reason. Through reasoning with each other we can discover the reasons for our discontent. If we determine the reason, we can determine the season and what we need to change. If I'm in the summer season, then I don't need a winter coat. But we have to determine the season first—the reason why we do the things we do. When we do this we can begin to assess the hurdles in a logical way that will help us solve the issues instead of putting them on the back burner.

The best answer is often to sidestep the argument. To evaluate the problem and figure out if it's a mountain or an anthill. Squash the anthills in your own brain; don't let them fester! There are far more important things in life to stress about.

But sometimes the issue really is a mountain. Small things may be indicative of greater issues. Talk them out. Set your problems on the table and reason them out together. Open expression and communication is important; and sometimes solving an issue is as simple as voicing it out loud. *No one can fill those of your needs that you don't let show.*

If simply talking about it still leaves you unsatisfied, perhaps you should try a trade-off.

Make the Tradeoff

Let's say John consistently leaves his socks on the floor and it irritates the heck out of his wife. She is sick and tired of picking up his dirty, smelly socks. Now if she knows John well enough, then she knows what might happen when she shares her irritation. She might know that if she shares her frustration with John, it will progress into a two hour argument. She then has to ask herself, *Will this tick Johnny off if I say something? Because it's already frustrating me and I need to find a resolution.*

One way to approach this issue is for her to simply pick up the socks. Saving herself from the stress and frustration and realizing this is a small anthill of a problem, his wife might figure, *Rather than arguing with this knucklehead of a man, and putting myself out, I'm just going to pick up the socks and get on with my life.*

Another approach is to vent her frustrations in that two-hour argument. She might get out what she wanted to say, have peace that she's said her piece. But at the end of the day, she's raised her own blood pressure and

John's, and the socks are *still* on the floor.

But, if he's a sweet-loving husband who she knows would do anything for her, she might try a direct approach, "John, honey, I'm working hard to try to keep this house clean for you. But I need your help. Would you pick up your socks?" And he might say "Darling, anything for you. I want your yoke to be easy; I want your burden to be light."

But if John has the habit of dropping his socks out of selfishness and inconsideration and he believes it is solely her job to be the keeper of the home, she may have to deal with him in a different way to overcome her objection of the socks. She might have to try a diplomatic approach by saying, "Honey, is there something you would like for me to do better to help make you happier?" And maybe John will say, "Yeah, baby. I've been meaning to tell you this for a while. That fried chicken ain't cooked done enough. It tastes good, but it just isn't cooked all the way through. I'd love it if you could just cook it a little bit longer." Instead of becoming defensive about the chicken, the wife could say, "Honey, I'll tell you what? I'll trade you cooking the chicken more for you picking up your socks."

That's a tradeoff.

Or John's wife might say, "Honey, I'm working; you're working. Why don't we call somebody in here to help us keep the house clean? We need to set it in the budget because I don't want to argue with you about something silly like socks on the floor. And I can't do it anymore, and you don't want to do it. So let's help ourselves out since we both like a clean house. Let's call Molly Maid® and let her do it. And we can spend the time we would have spent arguing or cleaning, doing something together."

That's a tradeoff.

Tradeoffs are part of the solution-thinking that is important for couples to put into play. The tradeoff game is a wonderful way to share and release stress. You may discover things about your mate and yourself that you didn't know before.

Tradeoffs are valuable in every facet of married life, not just in terms of cleaning. Money management, intimacy, time management, childrearing, and methods of communication can all be improved by making tradeoffs, and through the sharing that the tradeoffs encourage.

Break the Ice

Now, sometimes an argument is unavoidable, and then you have to figure out what to do when tempers run high. When tempers run so high that icy walls are erected between mates, we have to figure out how to break through the ice. Icebergs are pretty in the poles but not in our bedrooms and households. The best way to melt ice is with warmth. Be warm and kind until that ice melts away.

My son and his fiancé were having problems one day, and they weren't talking to each other. She approached me and asked me what to do to get through to my son. I told her to go over and kiss him. Kiss him until you break through. No matter what he does, just keep kissing him. So she did.

She kissed him. And he fussed. She kept kissing him, and he started to blush. And she kissed him some more, and he started to laugh. And then he couldn't help the smile on his face. They found a way to laugh with each other, which helped them get through the trouble they were facing.

Now the kissing might not work in every situation, but find a way to break through the ice with warmth, compassion and understanding. Heat your mate with love until that ice breaks. Shower them with the attention they deserve.

3. *V – Value Your Mate*

Compliment[1] and Complement[2]

Ephesians 5: 22–28; 31

22Wives, submit to your husbands as to the Lord.
23For the husband is the head of the wife as Christ is the head of the church, his body, of which he is the Savior. 24Now as the church submits to Christ, so also wives should submit to their husbands in everything.
25Husbands, love your wives, just as Christ loved the church and gave himself up for her 26to make her holy, cleansing her by the washing with water through the word, 27and to present her to himself as a radiant church, without stain or wrinkle or any other blemish, but holy and blameless. 28In this same way, husbands ought to love their wives as their own bodies. He who loves his wife loves himself. 31"For this reason a man will leave his father and mother and be united to his wife, and the two will become one flesh."

Marriage is that relation between
man and woman in which the independence is equal,
the dependence mutual, and the obligation reciprocal.
~Louis K. Anspacher

[1] An expression of praise, admiration, or congratulations

[2] Something that completes, makes up a whole, or brings to perfection.

I literally live for three things: 1) to please God, 2) to please my wife, and 3) to make my world a better place in which to live.

I know that there is nothing too good for my wife. If I have to give everything that I have to make her happy, then it's worth it. Matthew 16:26 reads "what will a man give in exchange for his soul, and what would he profit if he gained the whole world but lost his soul?" The valuing of your mate's soul should match that of your own. The Bible says "Greater love has no man than lay down his life for his friend" (John 15:13). My wife is truly my best friend, as she should be. And my whole life revolves around her. I can sit with her for hours and be content.

One night, we went out to dinner. Being a restaurant connoisseur, I always think I know the best places to eat, but this time she said, "Baby, I got a new place I want to take you to." Skeptically in my mind, (not to her, but in *my* mind) I thought, *Yeah right, she knows a restaurant* I *don't know.* But she took me to a steak house that was just off the charts! And I sat there with her for about five hours and we just enjoyed each other. Our food was done, people were going in and out, but we just sat there and enjoyed each other.

That's how relationships should be in marriage. You should be able to just spend the day together—no entertainment but each other. It's a beautiful thing when you can say, "Baby, let's just jump in the car and take a ride. Let's watch the sun set together" – when mates appreciate the time spent with each other, take every opportunity to talk with and listen to each other, and remember to experience the joy and wonderous value of each other.

Inner-Circle vs. Outer-Circle

Understanding the rightful placement of your mate as the top priority is something couples can easily forget. If your mate is in the outer-circle, you need to check your priorities. If my wife is the premier object of my affection beside God, she should not be in my outer-circle. I shouldn't get to her when I have absolutely nothing else to do. She should be first on the priority list. If I am forsaking all others and pledging my faith to her, that doesn't mean that I am solely forsaking females—I am forsaking *everybody*—male and female—because she has that paramount place in my life!

Jesus had an inner-circle as well as outer-circles. Jesus healed many people, but He only had twelve disciples. And within the twelve disciples, He had three that were a little closer. When He went through the Transfiguration, those three were there. When He went deeper in the garden to pray, He took those three. And to those three He gave specific assignments. He loved them best. Jesus did not trust just anyone to certain tasks; He held those three disciples in high esteem and asked only them to undertake the most important duties. For example, to John, He entrusted His mother (now you know you don't give your mama to just *anybody)*. Bestowing John the responsibility of His mother is clear evidence that John was a certified member of His *inner*-circle.

This same principle applies in marital relationships. Between wife and husband, there must be a demonstration of mutual importance over which no one and no thing takes higher precedence. No one should have preference over your spouse, not even your children.

We have to correctly arrange the priorities to be family-centric, and then ordered correctly within the family: God, Spouse, Children, the Church.

Sweet Talk (Be of Good Encouragement)

Now let's talk about expectations. Follow me here. I *love* to dress. My father was a dresser. When I go out and people say to me, "Every time you come out, you dress!" that causes me, while I'm getting ready the next day, to get myself together again! I have now established a reputation.

The same thing happens in relationships. When we compliment and praise our mates, we reinforce their positive qualities and encourage them to keep on doing the good things that they do.

If you say, "Honey, every time you get in that kitchen, you cook the best meals!" you are emphasizing the value of your mate's actions. By recognizing this value, you are encouraging your mate to continue that recognized behavior, to continue providing that special care. This expression of gratitude is something that many people have gotten away from. When you take your mate's actions for granted, when your expressions of gratefulness lapse, the perceived appreciation is diminished. Thusly, the spark in a relationship can sputter out and go cold.

Sometimes when my wife and I are out in public, I'll say "My wife is the most wonderful, most beautiful, vivacious woman. She is the french on my fries; the candy on my yams; the sugar in my coffee; she's all that *and* the extra bag of chips." And she'll say, "You're just saying that because we're out here in public." And I'll say, "Honey, remember when we're at home and you walk down the stairs in the morning, and I tell you how stunning you are? Remember when we're in the bed and I look over at you adoringly and I tell you how supportive and wonderful you are as a wife. Remember how I just hold you and tell you how much I thank you when no one is watching." I do those things more when no one is around.

There needs to be a consistency of encouragement, both in public and in private. When we appreciate what our mates are to us, when we show them and tell them how much we value their being, we reinforce the wealth of joy they bring to our marriage relationship and create a positive atmosphere of appreciation.

Psalms 107:2 says, "Let the redeemed of the Lord say so." We ought to see some sign that you are with the program; if the church isn't saying "Amen," the pastor starts to wonder if they're with him. Much of our culture is grounded in call and response; unless you give the call, you may not get a response. Your mate needs to hear that you adore them; when he or she does, the adoration will be magnified and returned.

We can make a difference in the heights our mates reach when we give encouragement and stand behind them. A young man within my ministry whom I have helped throughout the years married a young lady a few years ago. In fact, I opened my home up to them for their wedding where they were wed in my back-yard. His lovely young wife had been going through some rough times, but he continued to encourage her, to speak her value to her every-day, and she began to blossom. Within just a few years she rose in the ranks of her job to become the Regional Manager. His speaking her worth to her at every opportunity, remind-ing her that she is a wonderful woman, deserv-ing of the blessings of God, helped her reach higher heights.

When we serve each other dinner, or take

each other out, or chauffeur one another, or just bring each other coffee, we are acknowledging our mate's importance in our lives. We are expressing the significance of our mate's value as the top priority and premier confidant of our lives, as they rightfully should be, and the object of our highest earthly human affection.

The Art of Listening

Sweet talking is only one side of the coin, though. The other is sweet listening. Two of the greatest gifts we can give our mate are those of understanding and attentiveness.

When you are listening, you are not trying to tell your spouse what to do, or say, or that they are doing the wrong things. Sometimes, when we allow our mates to reflect off of us, they will find their own answers. To do this though, they need (we all need) someone to listen, to be a reflection pool.

We humans, oftentimes, like to listen to ourselves talk. We yak on and on. But in hearing ourselves, sometimes we begin to reason with ourselves and realize we are out of whack on our thoughts. We start to think *Maybe I ought to change that perspective and do my first work over.* You may not realize the power you have just by listening. When husbands and wives listen, they become the sounding board for each other.

The Bible says, "A wise woman builds up her house, but a foolish woman tears it down" (Proverbs 14:1). A wise person knows that they can win many of their battles, not by fighting and jumping to defensiveness, but by just being quiet. Now that doesn't mean you are tolerant of what's going. No. But, many a wise couple has saved churches and families by being patient, prayerful, reflective pools. And as we reflect the actions of our mates, God speaks to them through us. In the midst of that silent reflection, they will begin to realize their error.

I say this a lot, but, it's amazing. I can look over to my wife when I've said something or done something that doesn't seem quite right, and I look at her and see her countenance uneasy. It speaks back to me and tells me that I didn't say something right—I might need to check myself.

But if we look over when we didn't say something right, and our mate's fire off at us, a war starts. And no one's point gets heard. We try to talk louder, get up in each other's faces—we go to war. That's how we do. We try to tell each other off better than the other can. But at the end of the day, no one's opinion has changed. So who's won?

If at the end of the day we haven't reasoned together, everyone goes to bed with the same mindset. Then when the argument comes up again, the scenario is repeated until the time after that. Nothing is resolved. When we don't listen, the issues are never resolved, just continually recycled, even unto death. It seems we would rather continue to go around and around butting our heads up against the same walls than to resolve the issues.

Someone has to listen to learn to solve.

Break the cycle of unresolved issues, and listen to put things in the proper perspective. Listen to show how much you value your mate's point of view, knowledge and understandings. Listen to learn.

Fight the A.D.D. Cycle

But then sometimes, we think we have learned it all and get bored. Listen. When we first get here, we are babies. Then we call ourselves growing up. And when we get old, we return to being babies. They change your diaper when you are an infant coming into the world, and, if you are lucky and live long enough, they change your diaper when you are on your way out. It's amazing. Someone has to feed you when you are a baby; when all of your grinders are gone you have to gum on your food again like when you were first learning to chew. We go through cycles.

We peddle our way from one end of life to the other. Sometimes, during the trip, we forget who we are and why we are doing what we are doing. I have a saying: *I'm just a french fry in a world of potato wedges, trying to get to the catch up (ketchup) so I don't get caught up*. But it's so easy to forget our goals, our motivations, and the big picture. We get so bogged down in the daily issues and problems, that we forget the unbelievable beauty and overwhelming goodness in our lives.

Getting caught up isn't a crime. But getting

stuck in the cycle is. When you find yourself bored with life, jumping from pillar to post with no rhyme or reason, when you don't stop to see your reflection in the mirror, and you don't look into your spouse's eyes to say "Good morning," you are in the A.D.D. Cycle.

Attention Deficit Disorder (A.D.D.) is a persistent pattern of inattention and impulsiveness. Think about that now. A persistent pattern of *inattention* and *impulsiveness*. When you didn't notice that new dress or the fresh haircut—inattention. When you went out and bought that washing machine or car without consulting your spouse first—impulsiveness. When you forgot your anniversary or the big game—inattention. When you took that fine, flirty person's number just to boost your ego, *but it doesn't mean anything*—impulsiveness. It becomes a disruptive and divisive behavior.

You've got to get that A.D.D. in check. It's a common cycle that couples go through—when the newness of the relationship has worn off and you feel that you know each other to the point of boredom. *But it is a cycle.* One that you can cycle out of and avoid. That sweet talk that we talked about earlier not only encourages your mate but also helps to keep the home fires burning. Knowing that s/he is appreciated at home will keep your mate coming home. When you get an itch, think about who you want to scratch it. If it's the clerk in your favorite mall store, or the cute cashier in the supermarket, the co-worker in the next cubicle or the steering wheel of your car, then maybe you need to wonder why it's not your spouse. What's the problem? How can you fix it?

The feeling of being undervalued, unappreciated, undesirable, and/or unwanted can be crushing and hurtful. And when we feel that way, we often want to inflict that same pain on others. Try turning that tactic around. When you start to feel that impulse to go elsewhere to find your joy, when you start losing interest in your life at home, *jump* start your interest. Find that special thing about your mate that used to light your fire, and stoke it. Talk that sweet talk, stroke his hair, give her butterfly kisses, do SOMETHING together.

The only way to fight the A.D.D. feeling is to find the value of your mate again. Once you get married, the kissy-fishy stuff eventually wears off—like with a new car.

When people first buy a new car, they say "Don't eat in here," "Don't drink in here" and "Wipe your feet off before you get in!" But after that car gets a few miles on it, you find french fries on the floor and gum stuck under the seat. You'll find that car is not treated like it was when it was new. After awhile, if you don't wash the car, if you don't maintain it, you find yourself saying, "Man, I need a new ride."

Like a car, relationships require maintenance. If you want to expand your range, every now and again you have to have a fresh oil change; you have to change that oil if you want to keep the engine running smooth.

Sometimes escaping the A.D.D. can be as simple as making a cup of coffee. My wife is a coffee person; if she doesn't get her coffee in the morning it's like she's been deprived. But she knows I don't drink coffee every morning, so she'll get up and make herself one cup to get her groove on—and she's ready to rock and roll. If I wake up first, I'll go and make her that cup of coffee. It gets her ready for the world in the morning; and I just want to make sure that she has what she needs to get her engine started. If that's what she needs, I say let's crank it up! It's something as simple as a cup of coffee that will put a smile on her face, a caring kiss of thank you on my lips, and her happy walking out the door to face the world in the morning and eager to return home to my arms at night. A simple gesture, that keeps our home fires burning.

Spending time with your mate during that morning cup of coffee is quality time. It is an integral part of keeping the engine of a relationship revved. Make time for each other.

4. E – *Escape with Your Mate*

Just the Two of You

Ecclesiastes 3: 1–7

There is a time for everything
and a season for every activity under heaven:
2 *a time to be born and a time to die,*
a time to plant and a time to uproot,
3 *a time to kill and a time to heal,*
a time to tear down and a time to build,
4 *a time to weep and a time to laugh,*
a time to mourn and a time to dance,
5 *a time to scatter stones and a time to gather them,*
a time to embrace and a time to refrain,
6 *a time to search and a time to give up,*
a time to keep and a time to throw away,
7 *a time to tear and a time to mend,*
a time to be silent and a time to speak

To know when to go away and when to come closer
is the key to any lasting relationship.
~Doménico Cieri Estrada

Quality time is prioritized time that you spend with the people you love. But even quality time has to be prioritized, put in order. You have to make time for your family. I am a big proponent of family time—scheduling a family outing once or twice a month, sitting down together and sharing discussion over the dinner table every night—these are activities that are important for maintaining the balance of family life and building that family bond.

At the same time, you must also remember to schedule time for yourself. It's hard to fill the cups of others, when yours has run dry. So you have to make the effort to pamper yourself, to be still with yourself and listen to your own thoughts. Remembering that we are always changing, it is important to stay in touch with your own desires and needs. If you don't make the time for yourself, to get to know who you are and what you want, you can easily get lost within yourself and within your relationships.

But before *family time* and right after *you time,* you have to have *couple time*—a time that is set aside only for you and your mate. The atmosphere you create with your mate will determine the health of the relationship you produce. Create an atmosphere of love, sharing, and openness for just the two of you to enjoy.

Date Night

I was in the barber shop one day, and the barber sat down and said "Pastor, I'm having problems with my mate. Every time I turn around, she's all over me because I hang out with the boys." And this is how I replied:

"Well, she's trying to tell you something. You gotta listen. She's trying to say to you, 'I want you to show me I'm a priority in your life.' And you're not hearing that because you are so caught up in what *you* like to do that you are really placing her lower down on the totem pole than where she should be. You give all the boys a night but you never give her a night."

So I shared with him my secret—show her she is a priority by giving her a special night out, just like you do with the boys.

This quality time away is needed for intimate prioritized bonding and to reinforce the marriage value! This special time for just the two of you gives credence to the importance of your marriage.

Well, I went back to the barber shop and the barber told me, "Pastor, I did what you told me to do. I set a night out for her every week." He said, "All those arguments about the boys stopped. As long as she knows she has her date night."

I counsel the couples in my church to set time aside for just the two of them. I say to the husbands, "Date your wife *at least* once a week." Set a date aside; but it can't be the day that your football games come on, because no matter where you take your wife, you'll be thinking about the game. You'll be in the restaurant positioning her with her back to the television screen so that you can stare into the TV set, and not into her eyes. And you'll say you are out with her, but you aren't really paying attention to her, you're watching the game. That just won't do.

And I say to the wives, it can't become a time for you to talk about the kids or your job or your girlfriends. Because then you are still concentrating your efforts on things outside of the two of you.

I try to explain to my male congregants that women love to know that their husbands set that priority time apart for them. And they love to tell their friends, "Oh, I can't go out with you Friday night. That's my special night out with my honey." Other women just envy them because they can't get their men to give them a specific date night. But if you are giving your woman her date night out as well, she feels just as special and loved. She's not going to say to her girlfriend, "Well, why can't I find a man like that?"

Likewise, if you are giving your wife the attention she deserves, you will never be able to forget why she is so special to you. You will have her at least once a week all to yourself, reminding you who you feel in love with and why.

Creating quality time and reigniting the spark of passion is just that simple when it becomes a priority for you.

E.S.C.A.P.E.

As you may have discovered, I find acronyms to be helpful for remembering important information. So, just as we have broken down the four elements of L.O.V.E., I want to expand upon the principles of E.S.C.A.P.E. Consider the following six things when planning your escape.

ESCAPE

Make your escape an Event!

Agree on it. *How can two walk together except they first agree? (Amos 3:3)*

Plan it. *Failing to plan is planning to fail.* It takes much of the pressure off of the event if you know where you are going, when and how. It eliminates all of the guess work so you are free to just enjoy the time away. God is in the details, allow him to help you get organized and your escape is bound to be blessed.

Talk about it. Build the excitement. Make it something to look forward to. Anticipation is the seed that blossoms into pleasure.

E**S**CAPE

Slow down!

Don't make your escape like the dry cleaners—in by 11, out by 2. Your escape should not be a sprint—*Remember the race is not given to the swift, nor the battle to the strong; but to he that endureth to the end. (Ecclesiastes 9:11; Matthew 10:22)* Understand that marriage is a lifetime marathon; run it with patience, for the bible declares that with patience you possess your soul. Don't let the rat race of life rob you of the joys of private time with your mate.

Give yourself time to experience the grandeur of the moment. Slow down, smell the roses and enjoy the aroma of love.

ES**C**APE

Consistency.

Don't allow your escape to become irregular and don't allow the frustration of time apart to keep you from enjoying your time together. Make and keep your dates. Plan weekly time with your mate. It will open better channels of communication and help you develop a better understanding of each other's lives.

Regular meetings with your mate will stimulate the mind, body and spirit. You will find your joys enhanced, obstacles overturned and the frustrations with inactivity and stagnation eradicated.

ESC**A**PE

Create a comfortable atmosphere.

Where there is chaos, order will be absent; where there is order, chaos will be absent. The atmosphere you create will determine the outcome of your escape.

If it's romance you seek, set the mood with a candlelit dinner of you and your mate's favorite foods, soft music and the aroma of sweet incense.

If you need the rejuvenation of quiet time, try a handheld walk down a quiet beach, or sipping lemonade in the backyard as the sun sets, or taking a stroll in the park at dawn.

Or, if you need to get the adrenaline pumping to wake up your senses, plan an exciting, action-packed movie night that will energize both of your imaginations.

Your frame of mind is directly affected by

your environment. Set the scene that will bring you and your mate the most pleasure. Whatever it is that you need—peacefulness, romance, innervation, adventure, inspiration, enchantment—be creative and personalize the atmosphere just for the two of you.

ESCA**P**E

Prioritize your escape.

Emergencies happen, but don't allow any and everyone to keep you from your planned escapes. For your escape to be effective, it is imperative that you, your spouse and others recognize the time as a priority.

Reschedule other events, when possible, around your escape time. Set reminders so that you don't absentmindedly make conflicting appointments. Remember that this is an event! Just like you wouldn't miss that concert you paid $100 for the ticket or that Pistons (Bulls, Cowboys, Dolphins, Yankees… whatever) game, don't allow yourself to miss out on your together time with your spouse.

After your relationship with God, your relationship with your mate is paramount. God's word declared that the marriage relationship takes such precedence, that it causes a man to leave his father and mother and cleave to his wife. Now that is prioritizing! Walk in the example that God has given us. Prioritize your mate's happiness and experience the fullness of life that the Lord has intended for each one of us.

ESCAP**E**

Enjoy the time you spend together.

Life is filled with so many uncertainties. Realize that today is a gift from the Lord, that's why it is called the present. Don't let the joy of this moment slip through your fingers. Regret is a poison of the devil. Tell that lurking Satan to get back! Live every moment as though it were your last with the person that you love—without limits, without barriers, without end.

Small Pleasures, Great Treasures

There are many ways to escape. The weekly date is just one set time. But you can escape with your mate everyday. Early morning coffee, late night debriefings about your day, or stopping to watch the sunset on the ride home from work together—there are a million ways to take advantage of just the two of you spending time together.

Creating that atmosphere of intimacy and closeness can be achieved every time you and your mate are together. Even in a room with a hundred other people, you can escape with just your mate. When a husband opens the door for his wife and she says, "Honey, you are such a gentleman. Thank you for opening the door for me"—every time you perform that ritual, you have created a time for just the two of you. It is a communication between mates and no one else. You have both expressed your mutual enjoyment in and respect of each other.

When my wife cooks me chicken wings, I tell her, "Wife, you cook the best wings in the whole world." And when she watches me taste them and sees the joy in my face, we have created another moment that is just ours. She has honored me by cooking one of my favorite foods and I have honored her with my extreme appreciation. It becomes a ritual, an escape from the problems and the headaches. It has become a time in which we enjoy each other and the benefits of living our lives together.

Whether sipping Kool-Aid® together on the back porch, reading the newspaper to each other, sharing quiet kisses in the hallway, or rubbing your mate's feet after a long hard day, find time to be together. Make room for intimacy. Intimacy does not solely refer to intercourse. Being intimate means finding the innermost, essence of your relationship. It means becoming a confidant, a close friend familiar with your mate's deepest nature. Intimacy is the expression of your closeness and your bond. Knowing the way your mate likes to be kissed or touched, preparing that perfect meal, planning that perfect trip. Those are all expressions of intimacy.

Finding those small pleasures, those brief moments each day to touch base with each other, to be intimate, will fortify your relationship. And a strong marriage is a rare treasure. Most people go through life just thankful they don't hate their spouse, when they could be enjoying the bountiful harvest that God intends for us all.

5. Loving the Change
Enjoy Your Epilogue

Psalms 59: 16
I will sing of your strength,
in the morning I will sing of your love;
for you are my fortress, my refuge in times of trouble.

What is Faith? To be faithful?
To be full of belief that this marriage is going to make it.

Comfort is borne out of understanding. To be your mate's fortress and refuge is to bring a level of comfort that no other being on the planet can provide. However, to love through change and adversity requires courage and commitment. It is not for the faint-hearted or the weak. It is a significant undertaking to cultivate a relationship, to accept responsibility for your own actions and their effect on your mate. It is a leap of Faith. But many practical actions can bolster you on this faith-based journey.

Educating yourself about your spouse is the first and most important step towards a life of happiness. "If you don't know me by now, you will never, never, never know me, ooooh." Harold Melvin and the Blue Notes sang very true words, but there is hope to change that outcome.

Prioritize responsibly. Make it a matter of precedence that you get to know your mate; that you place your mate first in all earthly things; and that you show your love and appreciation for your mate unfailingly.

Communicate who you are and what you need, as well. Let your mate see you and know who you are. Try to listen and speak out of love and compassion. Remember, you catch more bees with honey than with vinegar. More resolutions will be made with sweet words than in bitter battle.

And bear in mind, everyone and everything changes. The world doesn't stop spinning, the seasons never stop changing, and we all grow older. It's a blessing. If you don't grow and change, you die. And while I am excited to meet my maker one day, today, I live for loving my wife.

Learn your mate.

Overcome obstacles with your mate.

Value your mate.

Escape with your mate.

Above all else, LOVE.

My Prayer For Your Marriage

Gracious, Everlasting Father, thank You for the wisdom and insight that You have allowed me to impart in this book, to encourage the members of the body of Christ to enjoy the blissful joy of happier marriage. I pray that the words that emanate from the pages in this book will find fruitful resonation in the hearts of every person seeking a happy marital union. I pray that it will lead to greater understanding of their mates, and a greater resolution to overcome the obstacles of this life together in cooperation and love with their mates. I pray that it will lead to a greater appreciation for the wonderful value their mates bring to the marriage covenant relationship. I pray that, by your grace, this book will be a loving catalyst that will lead married couples to years of intimate and joyful matrimonial bliss. And I pray, Father, that Your hand of tender mercy, will rest, rule and abide in every fiber of the lives and spirits of those reading this book and that they would seek to serve and worship You in the true beauty of a holy and sanctified married life through Christ Jesus, our Lord.

Amen and Amen

Quintin and Queen

My Personal Testimony

About the Author

It is a natural inclination for people to be curious about other folk. I enjoy listening to the testimony of others. There is always something new to learn about the goodness of God through the lives of his children. I try to be a man of action and service—less talking and more walking. But there is a time to tell. So I'll share my story with you here, prayerfully faithful that it will be a blessing to someone.

My father was a minister and his father was a minister. I'm not sure what great-granddaddy was doing, but a host of uncles and cousins are also men of the cloth. One uncle says, "Looks like preachin' runs in this family. But I hope it ain't just runnin', but that we're doin' it cuz we wants to be saved." I believe that many things are passed in the DNA, and living for Christ is in mine.

At the age of three, I used to sit on the preachers' laps in the pulpit. I would hang around these older gentlemen, my uncles and father, I don't know why; perhaps for the security and the wisdom. I developed a two-line sermon from hanging out with the preachers. They would call me down on the banister in the house when they had company and say, "Son, go ahead and preach." And I'd pull out my two line sermon and I'd say in my best preaching voice, "*God* is *up* and the *devil* is *down*." That was my whole sermon. But it was declared, "That boy is gonna be a preacher."

Most of the things that happened to me in my life happened on biblical numbers. At the age of twelve, I was directing the adult choir. I directed with every part of my body, my head, my feet, my hands, my spirit. And at that tender age, the Lord spoke to me, decreeing I would one day pastor that church.

At the age of fourteen, our musician left and we didn't have anyone to play the organ for us. So, I volunteered to play and learn by ear; now 38 years later I still play.

After high school, I attended C.S. Mott Community College and began a secular career in sales and marketing, in which I was actively involved for over 30 years. I have been blessed to work for major industry powerhouses, including General Motors, Nabisco Foods, and AT&T. Those experiences continue to benefit the glory work that God calls me to take on, preparing marketing campaigns for the Lord and advertising for his Church.

Then at 25, I publicly acknowledged my call to the ministry and began preaching. My first sermon was from Revelations 20: 12–15, which describes the Book of Life being opened and those whose names are not found in the book being condemned to burn in the fire and brimstone. My text was "Where are your reservations and who is your travel agent?"

At age 30, I became an ordained minister. Then at 33, I was introduced in the choir one week and the Lord spoke to me again, telling me that the next week I would be pastoring. I began organizing with seven or eight members who broke away with me to form a small congregation we named New Life Tabernacle Church of God in Christ. Providence found us a space in which to have service that served us for a year.

Near the end of that year, I spoke with a parishioner, a young woman whose son was running the streets. One Saturday night, she said to me, "I'm having problems with him, would you talk to him?" I told her to put him on the phone. The conversation went like this:

"Hi, Pastor Marshall."

"Hi, son. How are you doing?"

"I'm doing fine."

"The Lord told me that if you don't get back in church right now, you are not going to make it. This is an *immediate* call. God has a call on your life and you have got to move *now*."

The young man said "Ok, I'll be in church tomorrow." But when the next day came, he didn't show up. Twenty-four hours later, he walked into a drug house and was shot dead, at age 14.

Now I was in the middle of a building that would not accommodate a funeral and I needed a place to hold the service. I remembered that God had decreed I would become the pastor of the church of my youth. So I called and it turned out that the old church building was vacant.

I asked to rent the church for two weeks.

When they said yes, I took all of our materials and moved into the church building, because I knew what God had told me.

That two weeks turned into a month to month rental. A year later, we made an offer on the building which was accepted. We purchased the building and paid it off. 2010 will be our 20 year anniversary, and we are still happily in the church building. God's decree then, as always, came to fruition. And he is still providing me with instructions.

In the midst of building a career and a new church family, my own family grew. I am the proud father of six beautiful and talented children: Quintin Jr., Quinice, Sylvie, Dion, Damon, and Dondric. While my first marriage was not an everlasting union, it gave me the precious gift of children. They are a blessing to me everyday, even on the trying days, and I cannot imagine my life without the joy they bring me. And not long after the founding of New Life Tabernacle C.O.G.I.C., I met and fell in love with my beautiful life partner, Queen Esther. She has enriched my life in more ways than I can express and her love is a continual source of strength and constancy.

With the love of my wife and children to support me, I have excelled through the ranks, going from a minister to an elder, to a pastor, to a superintendent of the Potter's House District of the Northeast Diocese of the Church of God in Christ. A C.O.G.I.C. superintendent is a minister that presides over more than one church; in total, I oversee three churches, including the one I pastor. I have been honored to serve in various leadership roles with the C.O.G.I.C. and other faith-based and community organizations over the years.

God has blessed me to be able to work with and represent the concerns of his people. As a visionary, I have been called by the Lord to many works. It leaves little time for sleep or rest, but His plans are larger than my own. When God shows me visions of things that will come to pass, I just go on and do it. Believing in His Word and the connection I have with Him, I have been blessed with many triumphs. He has seen fit to educate me in the ways that would best help me serve my community.

During my secular career of over thirty

years of Fortune 500 corporate experience, twenty-five of those years in marketing, I developed skills that have been a benefit to me as a pastor and to other pastors as well. In this age of glitz and glam, proper marketing is key for any endeavor to succeed; and God, in His infinite wisdom, put me on a path to market to His glory. In the last year, I have helped churches spread the Word of God through commercials, billboards, posters, and websites. We have been able to establish a network of publicity for Christ, connecting graphic designers and videographers together to provide the public with better access to the Church. We are implementing new methods of reaching out, of calling to God's people. And we are figuring out more ways to make it an interactive process.

In cooperation with others, God has also called me to help his flock as they return to the fold. I have been blessed with many opportunities and the Lord spoke to me and told me that there are many others who are in need of second chances. To this end, with a number of government agencies and church alliances, we have developed a reentry program for citizens coming back into the community after incarceration. Many former prisoners find it difficult to acclimate to life outside of jail, because they cannot find jobs and have no way of supporting themselves. So, we are creating companies to provide gainful employment to this growing population. They are not glamorous jobs, but honest work created to help make this community a better place in which to live.

Then, helping God's people increase their territory, we have implemented the Community Rent to Own Housing program in which those seeking to become homeowners are able to do just that. Acquiring properties through Land Bank, we restore and refurbish homes, then allow interested lower-income families to rent for three years; at the end of that period, they are given the deed.

We are also in the process of beautifying the community to inspire homeowners to maintain the upkeep on their properties and increase property and home values in our area. Our Right the Blight Community Housing Project will match the funds of homeowners who improve the curb appeal of their homes; providing equal funds, up to

$100, for the planting of flowers and shrubbery.

I am also proud to have played a part in the construction plans for a huge community center that we hope will be a staple of the area when it is completed, offering meeting space, an entertainment venue and activities for every age group.

In 2006, God called me to retire from my secular career. He said it was my season to be in the community full time. God has put it on my heart to help my congregation, other churches and pastors of the city, and the disadvantaged communities that these churches serve.

I have given my life over to God and he has brought not only me, but those around me, a mighty long way. None of the victories can I claim for myself. All the honor and the glory must go to God. Two of my favorite sayings are "Let us operate in excellence" and "In the House of Mediocrity, Greatness is known by its Absence." The excellence of the Lord has allowed me to rise above mediocrity and to achieve greatness, not for myself, but for the community. We have great things happening around us because all things are possible through Christ who strengthens us.

I thank God for allowing me to serve him and for allowing me to serve you. It is my sincerest prayer that this book has been an enhancement to the joy of your marriage relationship and that you will share it with others to avert the rising tides of divorce and dysfunctional relationships. May the Lord bless you and yours always.

Lovingly submitted,

Supt. Quintin L. Marshall, Sr.

For More Information

About the ministries and outreach detailed in this section

or

To contact Superintendent Marshall to schedule a speaking engagement, seminar or counseling workshop

Please direct your requests to:

New Life Tabernacle C.O.G.I.C.

4401 Selby St.

Flint, Michigan 48505

(810) 787-9757